COMMON DOG TRAINING

Snooping Around!

CADMOS

DOG TRAINING

Read
Learn
Understand

Martina Nau

Snooping Around!

Train your dog to be an expert sniffer

CADMOS

Copyright © 2011 Cadmos Publishing Limited, Richmond, UK

Copyright of original edition © 2010 Cadmos Verlag GmbH, Schwarzenbek, Germany

Design: Ravenstein + Partner, Verden

Setting: Das Agenturhaus, Munich

Cover photograph: Ulrich Neddens

Content photos unless otherwise indicated: Ulrich Neddens

Translation: Andrea Höfling

Editorial of the original edition: Maren Müller

Editorial of this edition: Victoria Spicer

Printed by: Westermann Druck, Zwickau

Printed in Germany

ISBN: 978-0-85788-200-4

Contents

A question of snooping ...

Snooping permitted? Why, of course it is! If by snooping we mean utilising the canine's extraordinary powers of smell, we're thus opening up a new world of discoveries where human and dog can embark on the path to becoming a successful snooper team.

First off, let's have a closer look at professional sniffer dogs. They co-operate closely with their humans, working as customs and police dogs, as hunting dogs, rescue dogs, as mould-detector dogs and mine-detector dogs. In each case, it is their excellent nose that allows them to become indispensible helpers. Yet almost any dog could theoretically carry out these important tasks – if it had been trained from early youth.

The stars among sniffer dogs include the Bloodhound, the Beagle and certain varieties of Spaniel. This doesn't mean, however, that other breeds or types of dog are inferior in the olfactory department. Even a dog with the worst possible sense of smell will still have the potential to awe us humans with its abilities.

Dogs are not just equipped with an excellent sense of smell, they also thoroughly enjoy 'sniffing things out'. That's the reason why we often have a problem out on walks, when our dog constantly sniffs anything and everything he comes across. Sometimes it can be hard for us to get through to them, so lost are they in their world of interesting smells. However, we can also take advantage of this passion for investigating with their noses – in other words, their 'snooping' can be of great benefit to them and to us.

This book covers a lot of ground and will suggest many exciting sniffing ideas to try with your budding snooper dog. We begin with some fun nose games, and move on to suggestions for interesting activities requiring longer and more structured training, using concepts similar to those used with hunting or rescue dogs. In particular, the elements about telling different smells apart, the 'blind retrieve', and 'dragging and tracking' will be useful for utilising the instincts of dogs with a passion for hunting.

As well as enjoying lots of fun and games, this training will also improve our dog's levels of calm and obedience. In addition, for working and mixed breeds in particular, an activity only becomes worthwhile if the dogs feel they are doing something important. We should therefore endeavour to give an air of seriousness to our dog's training.

Before we begin, we will take a further look at the canine's incredible sense of smell.

The dog's sense of smell

While the human olfactory organ is comprised of five million smell receptors, the dog – depending on the breed and type – has up to 200 million receptors. The surface area of a dog's nasal lining is about 85 to 200 square centimetres; a human's is only five square centimetres. If you also take into account that about ten percent of the dog's brain is reserved for the processing of olfactory information, you can imagine how much greater the dog's powers of smell must be compared with the human's.

Dogs take in a huge quantity of different smells simultaneously, filtering the interesting ones in order to pursue them further. When a dog follows a particular trail, he can smell microscopically small dead skin cells or squashed microbes, no matter if the trail is several hours or even days old. The micro-organisms' state of decomposition can tell him whether a trail runs from right to left or from left to right. He is able to smell such a scent trail as clearly as we would be able to see it had it been marked with luminous paint. Try to imagine that!

Nose work is extremely tiring for dogs. The high breathing rate involved – up to 300 times per minute – increases their pulse frequency and body temperature. This is exhausting for a dog so, particularly early on in his education, it would be advisable to keep the training sessions shorter in duration. You will, however, notice your dog's stamina and powers of concentration will improve steadily. This also has a positive effect regarding other aspects of his behaviour – for instance, you might notice an increase in his ability to concentrate on you, despite the presence of external stimuli. You might also find he doesn't get nervous or stressed as easily. This is because his brain, as well as his body, is becoming fitter and healthier.

When a dog follows a trail, he smells microscopically small particles.

Nose work makes a dog tired and content.

How does a dog learn?

The tasks our dogs learn when doing nose work are often difficult and complex. Not every dog learns the same things in the same way. While dogs who mainly rely on their eyes, such as pastoral breeds (think of a Collie herding sheep) will swiftly benefit from watching; 'action' dogs such as terriers often learn quickly by trial and error. Others – above all sensitive, emotionled dogs, such as Irish Setters – feel most comfortable and will understand quicker if the first steps of a new exercise are conditioned very clearly. Think a little about your dog, and try different training approaches to discover which approach suits. This is an exciting process, and at the same time will allow you to get to know him better. This will benefit you in terms of your everyday routine, because if you understand which training approach is the most appropriate for your dog, it will be easier and quicker to teach him new things. In addition, you will be able to find explanations for some of his (perhaps previously mysterious) behaviour. When we train a dog, however, we should remember that in stressful situations he may develop a 'block', which makes it impossible for him to learn anything. For this reason, you should avoid exposing him to too much stress. This can be triggered by external stimuli, such as the weather, certain smells or other dogs, but also if your dog feels under pressure simply because he doesn't understand what you want him to do.

There are many possibilities for rewarding a dog; treats are only one among many.

When doing nose work you should always bear in mind the rules for learning:

- Dogs learn with regard to a particular situation, and can only generalise after many repetitions.
- Any small changes in the training structure will always result in a completely new learning situation.
- There has to be a direct chronological link between the dog's action and the consequences of his action in order for him to learn to associate both with each other – in other words, timing is crucial. We have about one or two seconds in which to give the reward for it to be effective.
- Don't forget the secondary reinforcer, which could either be a clicker or a reinforcement word such as 'good'. This should be conditioned, so the dog understands it. You'll find further reading on this subject listed in the appendix.
- The best reward is always the thing the dog would like best at that one moment in time. This can (but doesn't necessarily have to) be a treat.
- Your verbal and body language should be unambiguous from your dog's perspective, to enable him to progress from simple tasks to more complex exercises.

- Dogs often try out whether something works or not. If it does, they'll repeat the action; if not, they won't. Make sure the action is either worthwhile for your dog, or not, depending on the learning objective.
- Chains of behaviour (as, for example, a search with subsequent marking or retrieving) are always structured backwards, because this way we can reward each behaviour individually by giving permission for the next behaviour to be carried out, the ultimate goal being the reward – which may be prey, treats or some other desirable thing.

Nose work: going by instinct

Let us consider the fact that in doing 'snooping' games, we are actually working with our dog's instincts. That's why nose work offers an ideal opportunity – particularly for bored dogs or those with a strong instinct to hunt – to happily tire themselves out while at the same time decreasing their urge for adventure and hunting. Nose work will address various canine instincts – the tracking instinct, the flushing instinct, the retrieving instinct, the mental and physical activity instinct – depending on which snooping task we set.

For the sake of completeness, we will have a brief look at the individual instincts concerned. Then it will become obvious what opportunities the various snooping tasks offer for utilising the dog's natural instincts (and help with problem behaviours).

The tracking instinct brings to the fore the dog's desire to pick up a track and follow it.

The flushing instinct requires the dog to work with his nose in the air without picking up a track. At the same time, the dog uses his eyes and ears.

A dog with a pronounced prey instinct doesn't just want to pursue his prey, but also catch it.

The retrieving instinct makes our dog pick up the found objects and carry them away. The aim of our training should there-

Working with the instincts, rather than against them improves obedience and the human – dog bond.

The longer a dog's nose, the better is his ability to smell.

fore be – if possible – to encourage him to carry the prey to us.

And finally, nose work also gratifies the dog's activity instinct, because our dog has to run, climb and crawl in order to find the prey object. This is great for particularly lively and vivacious dogs – they don't have to aimlessly rush around the countryside any more, but are required to use their brainpower instead in order to follow a plan towards a set goal.

All these instincts are addressed by the search tasks; after the training they will decrease for a short while, so that even highly instinctively-charged dogs discover a satisfying state of inner calm. And finally, training with the instincts rather than against them produces a deep bond between human and dog, which will, last but not least, lead to a more obedient dog.

Tips and tricks for expert sniffers

No matter what kind of snooping tasks our dogs are supposed to carry out, with the right knowledge you can help them to work quickly and with success.

Particularly when training outdoors, you have to take into account the wind direction, temperature and humidity.

Generally, working against the wind will assist the dog, but this may not always be what you want. We can use the wind direction to greatly influence his style of working, in a positive as well as negative way. As we shall discover, this is especially significant for the blind retrieve and for dragging and tracking work. The same applies to the strength of wind. Strong winds dissipate smells over a large area, and our dog will be more likely to search with his nose in the air. Slight winds will have the dog search with his nose on the ground. The higher the temperature, the more difficult it is for the dog to carry out his task, because these miniscule organic traces will decompose much quicker when it's hot; in addition the dog's nose dries out much more quickly. The greater the humidity levels, the easier it is for the dog to be successful in his search. You should offer your dog a drink at regular intervals to make up for the loss of fluids and to keep his nose moist for an improved ability to smell.

While observing your dog at work, you will discover some exciting things. Have a look at whether he is working with his nose to the ground, with a half-raised nose, or with his nose in the air. Does he walk in large semi-circles or small ones? Does he move swiftly away from you, or is he frequently 'asking' whether he is still going in the right direction? All this defines his working style, enabling you to better understand your canine friend in everyday situations too.

There is one other small detail you ought to bear in mind: older dogs and dogs with a very short nose have a diminished sense of smell. Pick stronger scents for them so they will still enjoy doing nose work.

Always send your dog off on a search from the heel position. This ritual will facilitate his work, while at the same time training his impulse control. This means the ability to wait calmly before the start of any working action, which also applies to other life situations in general – for example, not to dash off on a whim, but to wait for permission instead.

Training with scents

There are lots of possible scents, but not all are equally useful. Sniffing coffee, for instance, can be very unappealing to dogs. They also tend to have an extreme dislike for certain perfumes. Smells they do like include camomile tea; any type of meat or chicken broth, aniseed oil (very diluted) and 'game' smells. Artificial game aromas are available from fieldsports retailers. But beware – I would only work with these as part of an anti-hunting training pro-

From hotly desired to unpleasant: scents.

gramme, when the objective is to offer a dog with a pronounced hunting instinct an alternative to tracking game in order to convert him to more harmless smells in the course of his training.

When working with scents, remember some smells that seem normal to us might be unpleasant to the dog. In this case, don't be surprised if he doesn't want to sniff a particular substance, and instead tries to avoid this smell. If you're under the impression that your dog 'doesn't understand' or 'doesn't smell anything', the real reason for this might well be that a particular scent is too unpleasant or too strong for him.

When introducing a new scent, you should dilute it a little bit more with every subsequent training session. This keeps his interest levels high.

Training with game substitutes

Think carefully about whether you use hare furs, duck feathers or other types of game substitutes for training, especially if you want to avoid giving your dog ideas about potentially searching for these. However, there is one exception: again and again we meet dogs who come for anti-hunting training who can only work up any enthusiasm at all if game substitutes are involved.

Only train with a game substitute, if there is no other option.

For dragging and tracking, the dog should wear a well fitting harness.

Properly deployed, they often provide the only access to dogs with a strong hunting instinct. If you can do retrieving or nose work with such a dog, you have finally found something that will at least come close to offering an alternative to real game. However, before too long you ought to make sure that he will also get excited about hot dog drags and retrieving dummies, and use the game substitute as a mere bridging device. You can also use the game substitutes for dragging and the blind retrieve, about which we will read more at a later stage.

Additional help

When doing more challenging nose work with our dog, there are some training aids which we will need to use more frequently.

This includes the water bottle, which we offer to our trainee more often than usual because sniffing is thirsty work, and a moist nose is better at picking up smells than a dry one.

Treats are the perfect tool for motivating a dog during training. However, they should not smell better or stronger than the object that the dog is supposed to sniff out.

Apart from the short lead, we also frequently need a long one, and this should be a field or drag line. Depending on the terrain and the dog's speed, a length of about five to ten metres has proved most appropriate. Make sure that the lead's diameter reflects the dog's size and weight.

If you are using a collar, this has to fit the dog well; not be too loose, but not too tight either. You should be able to slip two fingers between the collar and the dog's neck.

A harness is a better choice than a collar for dragging and tracking exercises, because in this instance the dog is allowed to pull on the Lead. If he was wearing a collar, this would not be good for his health.

If your dog likes neither toys, nor standard dummies, as a last resort you can use a food dummy as a search object. Every now and again – as a jackpot – the expert snooper is allowed to help himself from the food dummy (with your assistance).

The eyes during nose work

Why is it interesting to know what a dog sees with his eyes, when we're dealing with nose work? It's simple: because our dog doesn't close his eyes while sniffing. If we want to achieve certain training goals, the dog's vision can either help or hinder, depending on how we structure our training.

Dogs are not completely colour blind, but see the world in a similar way to those humans who suffer from red-green blindness. They are able to see some blue tones, but to a dog most colours present themselves as black, white or grey.

By choosing a search object of a particular colour, you might be able to determine whether the dog will use only his nose, or whether he will use his eyes as well. For example, if you take a blue-green search object, our dog will find it – especially in the grass – by using his eyes. If, on the other hand, we opted for an orange coloured object, this would almost be invisible to him, and the dog would have to find it by

The eyes play a part during nose work as well.

using his nose. If we have our dog search for a white sock, we might put it on dark floor tiles, because a quick success would give him self-confidence early on. Later, we put the white sock on a white carpet, and our snooping ace has to deploy his nose.

We should definitely make use of this knowledge for doing nose work as well. In the cup game (see page 34), what good is it if your dog only ever lifts up the blue cup when searching for treats because it sticks out prominently next to the two brown ones? It's no good at all – so to begin with you should use cups which are the same colour. If your dog is already a seasoned sleuth, you can use one blue cup to lead him up the garden path, thus making his task more difficult.

It is also important to know that dogs primarily see objects that move, as they

prioritise anything that is in motion. We can use this in order to steer our dog's instincts. If a dog is highly instinct-driven and over-motivated during training, we don't throw objects that he has to search for later, but instead we slowly place the object on the ground while he's watching, or else we don't let him watch at all. But perhaps your training partner isn't in the mood for searching? Maybe he only has very weak instincts? In this case, throw the search object in a high arch trajectory into tall grass or behind an obstacle. In addition, you can accompany this action with a sound. The movement makes the object come 'alive'. You'll see his interest in it will increase in leaps and bounds.

Determine whether the dog will use his nose or his eyes, by choosing the correct colour for the search objects.

Object found – what next?

The question is always the same: what will our dog do with an object once he has searched for it and found it? There are a variety of different ways for marking it, depending on the dog's breed, type or preference, and also the size and type of the search object.

Anton has found the search object ...

'Show it to me!' – marking by sitting or lying down

If a dog doesn't like to fetch or retrieve, or when the search object is too large to be carried, a dog can mark it by sitting down next to it. So how do we teach him to do this?

We structure the search task as simply as possible. The distance to the search object should not be great. When the dog has found the object, we praise him first with a click or with our conditioned reinforcement word, then we say 'sit' or 'down', and finally we reward him with a treat. It is important to deploy our secondary reinforcer as soon as the dog displays signs of having found the object, such as eager sniffing.

... and marks it by sitting down.

Another training approach literally entices the dog into sitting or lying down: put a favourite search object in a place where he is not able to grab hold of it. You can suspend it from a tree or hide it under a carpet. Let him try and reach the object. At some point he will give up and sit down or lie down, and you should instantly reward this. There are two ways of doing this: Either he immediately gets a treat and is given the search object after that, or you skip the treat and give him his prey straightaway. Depending on the dog you should opt either for the first or the second approach. Afterwards, have him get up by using a release word. Pick a word like 'run' or 'free', which you will use regularly to indicate the end of an exercise to your dog.

'Tell me about it!' – marking through sound

If the dog is supposed to mark the found object through sound, we should initially train the sound marking separately, prompted by a word or a visual sign. This won't take long, if your dog likes barking anyway. Hold a treat in your closed hand, and take his favourite toy but don't give it to him.

If your dog makes no effort to reach the treat or the toy, move it from side to side in front of him, or – and this is even more effective – away from him and back

towards him. Always bear in mind: movement reinforces the desire to get the prey. Do tease him a little. Even if he initially tries other ways to get the object of his desire, he will bark at some point. As soon as he makes the tiniest sign or the quietest sound, give him the prey immediately, if at all possible simultaneously. Again, timing is of paramount importance. After repeating this a few times, your dog will have learned: if I want something in this situation, I will bark. Assign a chosen command to this behaviour as soon as he makes a sound – for example, 'speak' – the second he begins to bark.

If the barking can be called up regularly with the 'speak' command, you can use it as a marker for the nose work. This approach is the same as described in the previous chapter for marking through sitting or lying down. The dog finds the object, you praise him using the secondary reinforcer, you say 'speak', the dog barks, you swiftly walk towards him to make sure that he stays with his search object, and then you reward him there and then.

Once more the search object can be put in a place where the dog can't reach it. Now you wait for him to bark. You should definitely reward even the smallest bark to ensure that he will repeat this action more often.

Particularly when working on 'marking through sound', you should not forget to use a release word, enabling you to tell your dog that he should cease barking now.

Hunting dogs are not the only dogs that can learn to mark by pointing. (Photo: R. Maurer)

Pointing

Pointing dogs – such as the Pointer, Setter or the Vizsla – will mark game or alternative prey by 'pointing', in other words they stop in their tracks the moment as soon as they catch the scent, muscles tensed, while some may also raise a front paw. They may remain in this position until they are addressed or touched by their handler.

If you detect a tendency to point in your dog, you can take advantage of this natural predisposition. Reward any pointing as simultaneously as possible with the clicker or the reinforcement word, then go to your dog and give him a reward in the shape of a treat, and/or the search object along with a release word. This way, he learns that this means that he can stop pointing. As before, it is helpful to ensure that the search object is hidden in such a way that the dog cannot reach it without your help.

Introduce the audio sign for retrieving only when your dog retrieves reliably.

Fetching or retrieving

If you teach your dog how to fetch or retrieve, the possibilities for having fun and pursuing further training will instantly multiply. We are in favour of having our dog fetch or retrieve in a way that he will be happy to do. Some dogs frequently carry all sorts of things from A to B anyway. If you happen to observe this, just call your dog with a simple 'come' signal, go down into a squatting position, and when he takes the object somewhere close to you, praise him thoroughly.

If he doesn't really want to give it up, swap his prey for a treat or a toy of equivalent value. To do this, take the retrieved object calmly in one hand, without pulling or tugging on it, and hold a nice smelling treat in front of his nostrils with the other. The dog will open his jaws almost automatically. At the same time you say 'let go' calmly and kindly, take hold of the object and give him the treat. Afterwards – and this is the big surprise of the day for your dog – you return the object to him, turn around and walk away. In most cases, the dog will stare at you in amazement. Take advantage of this moment, and call him to you in a friendly manner. When he comes, go down into a squatting position, swap his prey for a treat, and give him back his prey. After repeating this two or three times put the object away (into your pocket or bag) and conclude the game.

Only add the verbal sign 'fetch' once your dog is reliably retrieving objects. Bear in mind that a dog associates all actions which are happening simultaneously with each other. That's why you should only assign the name 'fetch' to the retrieving of objects once he has mastered it almost to perfection, otherwise for your dog this term will also include any other funny little actions that he happens to be doing at the same time. But what do you do about dogs who don't ever carry any objects, or who don't voluntarily take anything into their teeth?

Idea number one: as before, work with his instincts – this time his hounding instinct. Throw a lightweight, portable object only a few metres away from the dog. Most dogs tend to run after it, and will briefly pick up the prey. If this is not the case, you can try a short, moderate tug-of-war game. Let the dog win the first time round, but carry on playing straight away. When you're in possession of the toy, throw it away all of a sudden. Almost every dog will run after it, and take it into his jaws, because for a brief moment you have reinforced his instinct. This is the moment when you call the dog with a simple 'come' signal. The rest is trained as previously described.

Idea number two: train with a food dummy. Throw it away, and when the dog briefly takes it into his jaws, go to him and let him take some food out of it. After repeating this a few times, he will hold it in his mouth for longer, and then also run around with it. Again, call him only with the normal call sign.

Idea number three: shape the retrieving action with a clicker, as long as you and your dog are already used to working with it. For this you initially award a click for a mere glance towards the object that is to be retrieved then, step-by-step, you make a click for approaching, briefly picking up, and finally fetching the object. Unfortunately, the precise instructions for this shaping would exceed our remit. You'll find a recommendation for a good book on clicker training in the appendix.

You should initially train all retrieval exercises in a closed room that is as small as possible, so that the dog can't run away with his prey. As he will surely approach you in some way before long, he should quickly be successful – even if he does it rather by accident and unintentionally due to the restricted space.

There's only one thing that matters: fetching is fun!

The Bringsel indication

If our dog has found something that is too large and too heavy to retrieve, we can teach him the Bringsel indication as a

Stina marks a search object which she is unable to retrieve with a Bringsel (small dummy). (Photo: M. Nau)

further marker. The Bringsel is a toy, often a small, oblong, robust leather dummy which can be attached to the dog's collar. Once our dog has found the search object, he is supposed to take the Bringsel in his jaws and run towards his human. Afterwards he guides him to the found object. How do we train this?

As a prerequisite, the dog should know the terms 'fetch', 'search' and 'let go'. Have him retrieve the Bringsel several times, briefly play with him using the Bringsel, and then attach it to his collar. Next have him search for an object. Pick a small object that your dog is used to retrieving – possibly a toy, or your hat – and lay it down so the dog can see and smell it, but is unable to reach it. If the search object is large and difficult to handle, your dog won't be able to pick it up either. He will jump around you, perhaps bark, he will turn towards you, but you mustn't react to this. In the meantime, the Bringsel is bouncing on his neck, flying around his ears. Because he has only recently retrieved it, he will take it into his jaws. Praise him for this by immediately using the clicker or a reinforcement word, call him to you, and give him a reward. If your dog doesn't take the Bringsel into his mouth by himself even after several searches, go to him as soon as he has found the search object, and have him carry it to your joint starting point. There you reward him.

Although most dogs will understand quickly what the Bringsel indication is all about, at the beginning they will try out other things too. For instance, if your dog takes the Bringsel into his jaws, as soon as he is heading off, stop him and say 'let go', recall him and send him on the search once again. React in a similar way if he fetches the Bringsel without having found anything. Say 'let go' in a friendly tone of voice, and send him off once more. Dogs enjoy learning via the 'trial and error' method. Allow him to do this, but also show your dog when he has got it wrong.

If your dog has got to the point where he has understood the principle of the Bringsel indication, you have to have him train it in many different situations and terrains, and with a variety of different search objects, to enable him to generalise it, and mark it confidently and correctly.

If you closely observe your dog during nose work, you can learn a lot about him.

Snooping games

Small snooping games provide everyday fun for those occasional spare moments. Whether out of doors or inside the home, during a walk or from an armchair – you can train almost anywhere and without much preparation.

The test for expert sniffers

The following little sniffing test, in the shape of a food trail, reveals to you how your dog works with his nose. You should do this on simple terrain, such as a short lawn or on tarmac. This is not about perfect dragging work, but rather about observing how your dog uses his nose. We can also see whether or how he tells different smells apart.

Show your dog a piece of a hot dog, and have him sniff it. Go to your chosen place (your dog should not be able to observe you there), and lay a 20- to 30-metre long hot dog drag using a line. You'll find more information about dragging in the chapter 'Dragging and tracking'. Lay out the hot dog at the finish, so he doesn't see it until he is standing directly in front of it. Put the dog on the drag's starting point and send him on his way. He will pick up the scent, find the hot dog, and eat it.

Immediately afterwards take your dog back to the place where he has waited previously. Make a new hot dog drag in a different location, and add a cheese or salami drag on top of it. Separate the two drags after about eight metres. Leave the old hot dog drag and lay the second drag at an angle of about 90 degrees leading away from the first. Put another piece of hot dog on the end of the hot dog drag, but don't put anything on the end of the cheese or salami drag. Get the dog, have him smell the hot dog, put him on the start of the drag and encourage him to search. If he follows the new drag, he won't find anything. But he will most probably follow the old one, because this smell had brought him success before.

So what can we deduce from this? The fact that dogs are clearly able to tell different smells apart, and that they think while they sniff. Last but not least, we discover they are fast learners, particularly if this is associated with a success at the end of the exercise. Maybe you'll also learn a little about how your dog works. Observe him closely while he's snooping. It will be helpful for future nose work.

Food search games

One of the most popular search games has a very simple beginning: the 'search the treat' game. Begin by taking a treat and having the dog sit down. Show him the treat, put it on the ground a few metres away, go back to the dog and send him on his way with a wide sweeping movement of your hand. At the same time keep saying 'search' in an encouraging tone of voice. Repeat this a few times, and then lay out the treats in such a way that the dog can't see them any more. After repeating it a few more times, go and hide it in the next room. At the beginning, use large, very visible and strong-smelling treats; later you can use successively smaller ones. Hide these in such a way that it will be increasingly difficult to sniff them out: under carpets, on chairs, under cushions, on a step, behind a lamp, under a newspaper, between two towels. Be creative!

Next, show your dog two treats, then ask him to sit down, and hide the treats. You will see how quickly your expert snooper will learn how to count. If you only hide two or three pieces, he will soon surprise you by only searching for these, and not a single one more. If, later on, you would like to keep him busy for longer, show him a whole handful. You already know: snooping is a self-rewarding activity. The more the dog sniffs around, the longer he will want to keep doing it.

Make sure your dog concentrates on you and his task before sending him on the search.

Then you can send him off with a large sweeping arm gesture.

The search for treats can be easily extended to include the garden, or during walks. At first, the many external stimuli may be distracting for your dog. Proceed slowly and systematically, exactly the same way as you did when you first started. Only increase the level of difficulty when the dog is able to concentrate, and is enjoying himself. Don't ever put him under any pressure, because you think he should be able to do this or that by now. It would be much better to use particularly nice smelling treats for a particularly hungry dog. Throw them in a high-arch trajectory onto a freshly mown lawn or a tarmacked car park – to be concise, make it as easy as possible for your dog. Once again, bear in mind: as soon as the treats go flying, the dog tends to run after them. Have him wait a short moment before you release him with the 'search' command. In addition, you have to take into account the wind direction. To begin with, the wind should always be blowing towards you, making things much easier for the dog; this way he will learn first of all to work with his nose in the air and in a larger area. Later, when you go for a side wind or a tail wind in particular, things will become more difficult.

This is a good way for getting into nose work. From now on you have infinite scope for variation at your disposal. Have your trainee snooper search for his food bowl, his chew stick, his stuffed Kong®, or his scent tubes. However, you always have to show him, what exactly it is that he is supposed to search for. If possible, always use the same word, for example 'look'. Soon he will happily give you his full attention every time you say this word, because he associates something exciting with it.

We can make it even more difficult for our dog if we hide the treats which we have shown him beforehand (or the food bowl, the Kong®, the scent tubes), inside a tin or a box with holes, and then hide the tin (or box) in turn. Now he has to find the tin and open it, before he can get to his treats.

At this point you could also work with a marker. If the dog is unable to open or fetch the tin, or the cardboard box, he has to mark or show us his find. You have already read about how marking is trained. It would be best to use a marker which your dog offers up himself, or will understand easily.

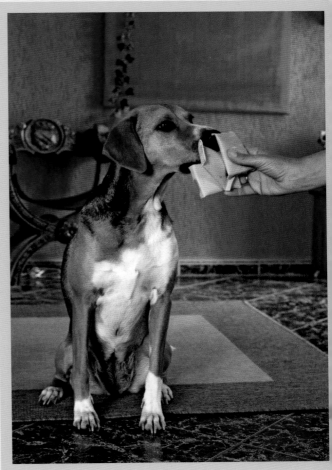

Let him briefly sniff the letter.

Packages with goodies everywhere!

This is another lovely variation. Collect the cardboard tubes from kitchen rolls or toilet rolls, and train your dog to fetch these with-

Choose easy hiding places at first, later you can choose more sophisticated ones.

Hide a treat under one of several similar looking cups.

Jasper is sniffing out the treat through some holes in the bottom of the cup. One cup is knocked over in the heat of the battle, but he only has a nose for the smell.

This smells nice! So that's where the treat is hidden.

out breaking them. Fill several cardboard tubes with a treat, and fold down the edges to close the tubes. These too he should bring to you without unwrapping them. Open them together, and your dog gets the goodies inside. This requires a lot of self-discipline on the part of the dog, but that can't be a bad thing, can it? Next, hide several 'packages' all over the house; under a carpet, on a shelf, in a corner – wherever you can think of. The dog enjoys the search, and we enjoy watching him as he is eagerly searching the whole flat for his 'red letters'.

Cup games – fun for dogs too

We're all familiar with cup games, where a person must choose under which cup an object is hidden, but did you know that dogs enjoy these games immensely too? And if there is fun to be had, we should not hold back!

You can also work with a marker for cup games. But it's obviously much more fun for our dogs if they can simply search to their heart's content, and if they are allowed to knock over the cups as soon as they have sniffed out the treat hidden beneath.

To start with, use two upside-down cups that are the same colour and have holes in the bottom. Plastic flower pots are ideal for this. They should have the same colour because dogs – as we already know – can only see a limited range of colours and should not end up being misled by them. At an advanced training level you can use just this limited colour vision in order to mislead him on purpose, for example by choosing two brown (neutral for the dog) and one blue cup (a recognisable colour for the dog).

Have your dog sit down to begin with, and put a treat under one of the cups while he is watching you. Then say 'search' and let him knock over the cup and have the treat. Of course this wasn't a proper search yet. All you want to make sure initially is that the dog knows what you have

planned for him. Repeat this exercise two or three times only. Afterwards, have him sit down again, put the treat under a cup, and shuffle the cups around each other for a bit. Just like a real cup game, this ensures the dog no longer knows which cup conceals the treat. Then once again, give the command 'search'. If the trainee snooper tries to simply knock over the cups without sniffing them, you have to hold onto them. Even if he now tries other ways to get to the treats: hold on tighter! At some point, he will sniff the correct cup. If this happens, lift it up immediately, or let him knock it over, and the dog is allowed to help himself to the treat.

No shortage of options – but which toy should the dog search for?

Once your dog is able find the search object under one of the cups every time, increase the number to three, four or even more.

Or, as a variation of this enduringly popular search game, you might use cardboard boxes instead of cups. Shoe boxes are the best, with small holes cut into the lids. Now you can hide a toy, treats or even his entire food bowl inside. You can decide whether you want the dog to lift the lid himself, or whether you want him to mark it. Just as before, the boxes should be identical at the beginning; you can increase the level of difficulty later by hiding the search objects in various different looking boxes.

'Find the duck!'

Our next search game is about learning some vocabulary, whith the simultaneous use of the nose. Our dog is supposed to

What is Anton looking for?

learn to identify a number of toys by their names and then to search for them. As a consequence, we have to hide the toys in such a way that he can't find them by just using his eyes. That would be far too easy – anyone could do that.

As a first step, the dog has to learn that the duck is called 'duck', and the ball is called 'ball'.

Begin by showing him the first toy; in this case it's a plastic duck. Say 'duck' at the same time and have him sniff it. Next, put the duck on the ground, point towards it and say 'search duck'. Your dog fetches the duck, or he marks it, and you praise him. If he shows no interest in the duck, when you're just putting it on the ground, throw it in a high arch trajectory and have him run after it, while at the same time saying 'duck'. After repeating this a few times, conclude this unit of training.

For the next step, have the dog sit down and let him watch as you hide the duck. Even at this stage, you should start to think of increasingly cunning hiding places. Make sure that your dog doesn't

Ah! His food bowl.

spot the duck first off, instead of sniffing it out from under a cushion for instance. Have him sit down, then hide the duck in a different room somewhere he can find it easily. You can ask him to go on increasingly longer searches as things progress.

Only repeat the training approach described above with a different toy once you have got to this point. Initially, let your dog search for this one thing only. Eventually, you can alternate between different objects, always in association with the relevant name. After a number of repetitions, why don't you put him to the test? Hide both toys at the same time. Will your dog really search for the duck when you tell him to? It can take a while before your dog can identify the toys by their names, but this isn't about a quick success, but about doing something together.

Once he is able to tell the two toys apart, you can add a third. Give this a name too, and train with it separately, without the two already familiar toys. Once your dog has learned the new name, hide all three toys at the same time, and after initially having him search for the new one, he can later randomly search for all three.

It would be a shame, however, if we let our snooping ace only search for unimportant things such as toys. How about teaching him the word 'glove', or perhaps the word 'scarf' and 'hat' a little later? If you drop your glove during a walk, you could carry on for a few metres, turn around at some point, and have your dog search for the lost object by saying 'glove'.

One duck, many places

Next, a nice variation of 'hiding our plastic duck': take the duck, and have your dog sit down. Now walk from one hiding place to the other, pretending to put the duck there. At some point you do put it down, but carry on pretending to hide it here or there. Visit several other hiding places in the same manner, only then go back to your dog and send him on the search.

Once you have put the duck in its hiding place, you should take care to control your body language. Your dog will instantly notice, if you keep looking towards the actual hiding place, or if you turn in a certain direction. Maybe you could run an experiment where you help him on purpose with a turn of your body or a clear glance in the right direction. You will see how well your dog can read you. Are you able to do the same vice versa?

'Search for the lead!'

Training on the lead can have a therapeutic effect on some dogs, while others don't like it at all, suffering stress whenever they are on a lead. If you have this problem with your dog, first of all you should teach him how to search for his lead on command. Initially it will not be easy to get him to like his lead, but that's the point of this exercise after all. Work with a clicker or a reward word, and a particularly nice treat. Plan several short training units spread out throughout the day.

There are two different approaches for reaching our goal. The first is based on shaping with the help of our secondary reinforcer; the second makes use of the dog's prey instinct.

For the free shaping, put the lead on the ground and initially reward your dog

Send your dog off to search for his leash with a large sweeping gesture. You should always use this same gesture when your dog is supposed to search an area.

for every glance he makes towards it with a click or a reinforcement word. Slowly he will move closer to the lead, sniff it, and perhaps even touch it with his paws or his nose. Reward every additional step that takes you closer to your goal. Be patient with your dog and give him time. At some point he will carefully or playfully take the lead into his jaws for the first time. Now he gets a jackpot reward, and you conclude the exercise. This training should be repeated in short regular units.

Training via the dog's instinct usually offers a quicker way forward. For this you should knot the lead into a ball making it easier for your dog to carry it. Get him interested by waving this 'lead ball' in front of his nose, then throw it (not too far) away. Encourage him to run after it immediately. This time, the objective is not a calm stationary stance, but first and foremost to have fun. Most dogs start off instantly and catch the lead as if by reflex. Don't wait until your dog begins to wonder what he is supposed to do with this strangely shaped object, but go down in a squatting position and call him with a 'come' or 'here'.

Only introduce the word for fetching the lead – for either variation of this exercise – once your dog fetches it reliably. Do use the same word that he is already familiar with for fetching, and just add 'lead', for example 'search lead' or 'fetch lead'.

Whether you plump for one training method or the other depends on your own tastes, but also on the type of dog you own. If he doesn't have a very great hounding or prey instinct, or doesn't like to fetch, the first approach might be better. But otherwise the second method will get you there more quickly. Simply try it out.

In due course, your dog will start feeling a lot more comfortable while on a lead, and will be better behaved as a consequence. I know of more than one former notorious lead puller or lead hooligan who was transformed in his behaviour on the lead thanks to this training. This conversion is always possible if the dislike for the lead is exclusively due to the dog's negative feelings about it, whatever the reason for this may be. Instead, from now on, you're telling him the lead means having lots of fun!

Of laundry baskets and suitcases

Filling suitcases or a laundry basket with clothes and hiding a toy or a treat in amongst them always gives rise to an interesting search task. Once again, the eyes are not in with a chance – our snooping expert is forced to sniff out his target. When he digs his nose into the laundry we can observe how he is taking in the smells while thinking it through at the same time, and how he is using his nose to sort through the laundry. Of all nose games, this one offers the greatest scope for having a good time.

Begin by initially showing the dog the object which he is supposed to search for. Take the opportunity to have him sit or lie down – which exercises his impulse control – and teach him the word 'sniff' just by saying it while he is sniffing the object. Then hide it while he is watching, mixing everything well together in the suitcase or laundry basket. After that go back to him, and send him on the search by saying the word for search and making that by now familiar sweeping gesture.

Socks provide a nice alternative to this game. How many times are we almost certain that we have put both socks of a pair in the washing machine – and for some inexplicable reason only one of them re-emerges after the wash? We believe that even a single sock deserves to have a useful task in life! Put a treat or a toy into one of the many socks selected for this task, hide it in amongst all the other socks, and send your dog on the search. Once he has found the correct sock, he has to fish out the prey as well. Be particularly watchful during this game to ensure that very greedy dogs don't swallow the whole sock with the treat

hidden inside. The smaller the sock is, the greater the risk that a dog on the brink of hunger might be tempted. Stay with your dog throughout and keep a close eye on what he is getting up to with the sock. This way, in an emergency, you will be close at hand and able to intervene.

Telling different smells apart

Telling different smells apart means, for example, you teach your dog how to find out which object was the one that you previously held in your hand; or to distinguish between tea and coffee; or to mark whether or not a certain smell is present. For instance, mould-detection dogs work along these lines, as do police and customs dogs.

Up to now, our dog has been searching with his nose for things that he had previously seen. He used both his eyes as well as his nose for this. Now he is supposed to learn how to search for something that he has only smelled, but not seen beforehand. From now on, he will only work using his nose. When he sniffs an object, he picks up many different smells. Now he has to achieve a mental masterstroke: he is supposed to remember the smells. For the second step, he will sniff a totally different object, and compare the smells of both objects. If there is a match, he is supposed to fetch or mark the second object.

Scent tubes

Scent tubes are small white tubes made of hard plastic, which have holes in them

Scent tubes

from which the most beautiful scents are emanating. You can fill them with treats or with other smelly things to be sniffed out (for where to source scent tubes, see page 77).

Although you could have the dog mark the 'correct' tube amongst all the different scent tubes, there are also a lot of additional ways of using it, provided that he learns to fetch or retrieve it. You could use it instead of a food dummy or a toy that you throw into the bushes or secretly hide in high grass, and have the dog look for it. The dog ought to be unable to reach the scent samples without our help. In addition, the tubes should smell almost neutral after careful washing, even after frequent use.

The search for scent tubes

Just as with fetching or retrieving food bags, there may initially be a small problem with having the tube returned because the dog may try to keep it to himself and open it.

This training provides a good first step into the work with scent tubes: put the treat in a tube, let the dog watch you doing it, and say 'sniff' while you hold the tube in front of his nose. This special training step is needed later for the differentiation of smells.

Next, you're letting him watch while you hide the tube. Then you go back to the dog and say 'search'. Support the word 'search' with a large, sweeping, encouraging hand gesture. Once your dog has found the tube, and has taken it into his jaws, go

down into a squatting position and call him. He should bring it to you. If he doesn't, remain friendly and go to him, open the tube and give him the treat. Even if he tries to open the tube, he won't be able to, because it is tightly sealed with a lid. Let him try for a moment (but not for too long – who knows, some canine smarty pants might manage it after all), then assist him. He will quickly understand that he won't be able to get the treat without your help.

Now you have a plethora of possibilities at your disposal for keeping your dog occupied with scent tubes, both indoors and out. You can use them for calm stationary exercises, either by throwing them, or having your dog wait a moment, and then letting him fetch it. Or you can hide several tubes and send your dog on a number of searches in a row. As a reward, you can either open each retrieved tube immediately, or you can wait until he has fetched them all, sit down on the ground with him, and turn the unpacking into a small ceremony.

Telling apart smells in different scent tubes

Scent tubes offer the perfect way into 'telling smells apart' for newbies. With the help of them, dogs can understand quickly what we're trying to achieve regarding the differentiation of smells.

You will need two tubes to begin with. Put a strong smelling treat into one of them, leaving the other one empty. Let the dog sniff the scent-filled tube and say 'sniff' at the same time. Hold the empty scent tube far away from him, and don't let him sniff it under any circumstances. Have your dog sit.

Now you lay out both scent tubes not too far away, so they are easily visible. Your dog is supposed to watch you doing this. Go back to the dog, stand next to him and say 'search' in a low but motivating voice, accompanied by a wide sweeping arm gesture.

When our expert snooper sniffs the correct tube, reward him with the clicker or the reinforcement word, and ask him to fetch. You have already trained this, and he will know instantly what you mean. If he brings you the tube, open it immediately and give him the treat inside. Make sure you don't let him fetch the empty tube, but go and get this yourself. After all, you don't want to confuse your dog.

Of course, you can also have your dog mark the correct tube, as opposed to fetch it. However, in addition, you should always make sure that the tubes are sufficiently spaced apart to make the marking clear and unambiguous.

After repeating this a few times, and once your dog has learned that the point of the exercise is to fetch the tubes smelling of treats, you can add a further empty tube. It's only now that things will prove difficult for your dog. In all probability he will need to repeat this a few more times, before he understands that he is supposed to sniff out the scented-filled tube this time round as well. The reason for this is simple: dogs learn in the context of a particular situation, and aren't able to generalise as quickly as we humans do. You should only add a further tube when your dog has mastered the exercise with three tubes. Or even better: before doing that you could pick treats that have a less intensive smell. Once the dog is able to tell the weaker smells apart, the number of scent tubes can be increased for the next step. After all, our dog is supposed to learn to concentrate on weaker smells as well.

Once your dog has started enjoying the search, it is time for a new challenge. Go back to using only two tubes. One should be empty and have a neutral smell, while you fill the other with things like noodles, rice, hazelnuts or a rag soaked with a scent. Let the dog sniff (using the word 'sniff') the filled tubes and put both tubes on the ground next to each other. As before, once he starts sniffing the correct tube, reward your dog with the clicker or a reinforcement word initially; later, you should let him make his own decision regarding which tube is the correct one.

From now on, when training with a variety of different substances and fragrances, you will have plenty of new ideas for further training options and variations. However, bear in mind there are scents a dog won't particularly like, while there are others that he might love. Every time you get the impression your training partner doesn't understand an exercise, or that he is unable to find the scent, it is highly likely that the only reason for his evasive behaviour may be that the scent is unpleasant to him. This is often the case

Lenny is given a filled scent tube to sniff. He picks up the scent and memorises it.

Then he has to stay sitting down, and watch the tubes being laid out.

He is only allowed to go ahead after he gets the command.

He concentrates hard on the search for the tube.

He fetches it, and is given a reward from inside.

Lost your keys? Following the word 'smell' Mary picks up her owner's scent from her hand.

Mary starts looking for the keys after she gets the command 'search'...

... finds them by the side of the path ...

... and returns them to her owner immediately.

when strong smells, such as perfume or coffee, are involved. By contrast, almost all food stuffs make very popular search objects, including spices such as aniseed or sugar. Sometimes a dog may just have a personal preference or an aversion – in which case you should swap the scent concerned for another one in order to find out whether he hasn't understood the exercise, or whether he just wants to avoid the fragrance.

Lost a glove?
No problem!

There are many exciting tasks that arise from the dog learning how to tell smells apart. We can have him search for something, either in the house or in the great outdoors. Meanwhile our dog is learning a completely new way of working. Instead of naming the object he is supposed to find, we let him take a scent sample from our hand. He is supposed to search for the object that smells of our hand.

Take a glove, for example. Have your dog sit down and then sniff your hand. Say 'smell' while he does this. He is supposed to memorise your personal scent. Lay out the glove not too far away, so the dog can see it, roughly indicating the direction with a wide sweeping arm gesture, and saying 'search'. Maybe this is the first search exercise you are doing with your

dog, and he just gives you a look of non-comprehension instead of heading off? In this case, walk a few paces towards the glove, and repeat the verbal and visual signs in an encouraging manner. Now the dog can either bring you the glove, if he is already able to retrieve, or you opt for a marker.

Repeat this step several times. On each occasion, have the dog sniff your hand beforehand. Lay out the glove increasingly further away, until you eventually hide it. To increase his confidence, you should let the dog watch you doing this a few more times. Finally, hide the glove in his absence. Now he knows exactly what he has to do. Mind you, he has only specifically learned to search for your glove. Now we have to generalise this action.

Pick some more personal objects. You could opt for a scarf, a shoe, the dog's lead, or your bunch of keys. Be warned, however, that many dogs don't like taking metal objects into their teeth and you may need to attach to your keys a small soft toy or some other object your dog already enjoys carrying around. Before starting with the training for smell differentiation, first have him carry the bunch of keys around, so he gets used to the way the keys dangle and the sound they make. Now you're ready to start. Repeat the sniff-search ritual a few times. Now you can 'lose' the objects during walks with your dog.

Fijari picks up the scent of a pine cone while his owner is holding it in his hand.

After the pine cone has secretly been put amongst the others, he is sent on the search.

Now he is supposed to sniff out the pine cone the scent of which he has picked up previously.

One pine cone among many

Nature offers us many opportunities for making going for walks more interesting. Leaves or pine cones look almost the same when they're lying next to each other, making them ideal objects for nose games. All dogs enjoy picking out the one that smells different from all the others. Pick one of the many pine cones off the ground, and take it firmly in your hand. Have your snooping artist smell it, and say 'sniff'. Distract the dog briefly, in order to make him look the other way while you throw the pine cone back on the ground to rejoin all the others. Then say 'search' and have him search. Remember precisely which pine cone is the correct on, so that initially you're able to praise him straightaway when he sniffs it. After repeating this a few times, you should let the dog work on his own.

He then gets a treat for retrieving it. If you are working with a marker rather than retrieval, it makes no sense to use sitting down as a marker for this exercise. Maybe you should train him to give the object a pronounced nudge with the best part your snooping expert has at his disposal: his nose.

Of course, you can train the same thing using leaves, acorns or other objects that look identical. Using rocks is not a good idea, because they're bad for the dog's teeth, and also some dogs tend to swallow them.

'Find the twin!'

There is one task that does not require much effort: soak two pieces of cloth or paper tissues with the same scent. Your dog is supposed to learn to search for the second piece of tissue, after you had him sniff the first one.

As before, the training sequence is structured in a simple and logical manner. Take both pieces of tissue in your hand. With the command 'sniff', let the dog pick up the scent of the first tissue. Then have him sit down, and visibly lay out the second tissue: this means your dog is supposed to watch you in order to see where you're putting it. You should hold the first tissue behind your back. If you wave it about too much, your dog will become more interested in that one, rather than in the one you laid out for him. Then you send him off on his search, once again with a wide sweeping arm gesture and the word 'search'. Now the dog can either retrieve the tissue or mark it.

Reward him with a reinforcement word or the clicker, as soon as the dog has touched the tissue with his nose.

There are countless scents available for this exercise. But remember not every dog finds all scents equally pleasant. He may not even pick up some tissues soaked in perfume, or he will ignore them during his search, while he may well devour one that has been soaked in brine. Adapt the scents to suit your dog.

After repeating the first step a few times, put the tissue to be searched for on the ground, where the dog's can't see it any more; but let him watch you while you're hiding it. Then send him on the search.

A few exercise units later, lay out the scented tissue before you begin the training session, have your dog sniff the second tissue, and send him on the search.

Advanced paper tissue sniffers can eventually work with two tissues laid out for them, one scented, the other not. Reward your dog right at the start, as soon as he sniffs the correct tissue – the one that is scented.

There are further possible exercises that are increasingly complex. Either you soak just one tissue, and lay out several unsoaked ones together with the scented one. Or you soak several tissues and hide them at the same time as you hide some unsoaked ones. The dog is supposed to pick out all the tissues that smell just like the scent sample that you have given to him previously. To begin with, lay out the tissues next to each other – later you can hide them in a larger area that the dog has to search.

The support dog for allergy sufferers

Do you suffer from allergies? Or perhaps someone in your family does? Even if this sounds rather unbelievable: almost any dog is theoretically able to indicate to an allergy sufferer whether the substance that triggers his allergy is present in particular foodstuff. Very often apples, strawberries or nuts can trigger dreadful allergic reactions. So the idea to make use of the extraordinarily capable nose of our four-legged companion and to train him to become our support dog is not that far-fetched at all. Take nuts, for example. What we're trying to achieve is to be able to hold a food that we intend to eat in front of our dog's nose, so he can examine it and ascertain whether it contains any nuts or traces of nuts.

Fill a bowl or a scent tube with nuts, and at the same time another one with a different food which you're a hundred percent sure does not contain any nuts. If you use a bowl, it would be best to cover it with some perforated foil, so your dog is able to pick up the smell, but can't eat the food. Send your dog on his way with a word command, such as for example 'search nuts' and let him have a good sniff at both containers. If he sniffs the nuts reward him immediately with the clicker or a reinforcer, afterwards he gets a treat. Your dog will soon realise: it pays to sniff out the nuts.

For the next step, take the nuts as well as some different foods that your dog

Anton sniffs the biscuit and ...

... lies down, thereby indicating that it contains nuts.

is now supposed to sniff. Sniffing the nuts is always rewarded.

Now our future life-saver has to learn a sensible marker. This could be sitting down, for example. It is a clear gesture which wouldn't be disruptive in a restaurant, for instance. Up to now we had our dog stand up during training. Let him sniff the nuts once more and say 'sit'. Initially use a single alternative smell, then several. While he is sniffing the nuts, keep repeating the word 'sit' over and over.

Once your dog has understood this, present him with a foodstuff which contains nuts, for example walnut cake, and another one that is nut-free, such as lemon cake. Train this in the same manner as before, and don't modify the previously adopted rituals. Once your dog is doing this without mistake, use a large number of different foodstuffs with or without nut content for your training.

Attention: make sure you proceed very systematically, and not too fast. Avoid over-large steps in your training. Work in a calm and stress-free atmosphere, and initially preferably alone with your dog to ensure he is able to concentrate well. Bear in mind that this is not just about a leisure pursuit, but that you are actually training

an assistant who may be responsible for the well-being of yourself or another family member at some point in the future. You will see that the relationship between you and your dog will improve further, because you're working together on an important project.

The blind retrieve

We have heard about extensive large-scale searches and blind retrieves in connection with the work of rescue dogs, as well as hunting dog. Rescue dogs carry out extensive large-scale searches in order to find missing persons, hunting dogs use them to track down injured game. The search for toys or treats in the chapter about snooping games has similarities with the blind retrieve, but it involves a rather more playful approach. In this chapter, we aim to teach our dog to search for several objects of a similar nature on his own and in a particular area. In a way, we are imitating a hunting situation, similar to what a hunter would experience together with his gundog.

It makes sense to pick objects that our dog is supposed to bring to us once he has found them. This way he has to use his hunting instinct in all its sequences, right up to the retrieval of the prey. But even dogs with a less pronounced hunting instinct like to carry their found objects around, because this is their way of enjoying their success.

This snooping discipline represents a perfect, enduring – and even a lifelong – occupation. We should train it systematically, and with a logical structure, which will enable both the dog and his human to experience fun and excitement.

Things you can search for

But what sort of objects can the dog search for? Personally, we prefer to work with dummies. These are little sacks stuffed with synthetic granules, which weigh up to 500 g and can usually float on water. They are available in different sizes and weights. Alternatively, you could also continue to use toys, food bags or scent tubes – again, use objects which share similar characteristics.

If the objective is to offer a dog with a strong hunting instinct a substitute for hunting game, as an emergency measure you can resort to 'substitute game', such as dummies made from hare fur, or game scents. However, in this case I would always try to back-train your dog to 'normal' dummies as soon as possible.

Dummies in particular have various different characteristics that can help you decide whether the dog should work exclusively with his nose, or whether he should rely on support from his eyes, in order to reach his goal quicker. This may be the case with dogs who either have very little instinct or a huge passion for game, or with very sensitive dogs. If we opt for blue-green dummies, the dog can see them

Even if you initially use game substitutes and game scents for your search training, make sure that you try getting your dog interested in other search objects as soon as possible.

better, learns how to search with his eyes as well, and therefore finds them more quickly. His motivation increases. Orange or olive-green coloured dummies, on the other hand, are almost invisible to him – meaning he has to use his nose. For us, in contrast to our dog, it should be especially easy to quickly spot the orange one, so for once we actually have an advantage over him in the seeking department. This would be a particularly good thing when dealing with a very self-confident dog. On the other hand, it could also be important to be able to give support to the dog in the search area in order to bolster his confidence. Of course the same goes for other search objects: the object's colour plays an important part.

Some dogs with a strong hunting instinct are unfortunately no longer interested in toys or simple standard dummies as soon as they're out in nature. In these cases, sometimes the only way to get through to them is to resort to substitute game. The end justifies the means. Make sure, however, that with a dog like that you soon add obedience and impulse-control exercises to working with substitute game, otherwise you might end up whipping up your dog's hunting instinct to such a degree that he'll embark on his own private hunt at any opportunity. If this is likely to happen, it would be wise to keep your dog on a lead on your way home, just to be on the safe side.

Jasper really enjoys searching the hare fur dummy. Always combine the work with game substitutes with obedience and impulse control exercises, to ensure that your dog will not start chasing real game, or maybe stop doing so.

We're searching in open terrain

When training out in nature we have to be aware of a few things. Depending on the dog's training level, we can either opt for simple terrain, or more difficult ground with varied vegetation and difficult-to-reach areas. In trickier terrain the dog should always work without a lead, collar or harness, to prevent him from having a bad experience as a result of injuring himself or getting himself entangled in his lead.

The weather conditions are also of great importance. Any type of extreme weather increases the difficulty of the search. If it's hot, or if there's heavy rain, snow on the ground or strong winds, this may be a good challenge for advanced snoopers, but for inexperienced beginners they will quickly become demotivated, either because they fail to find the search objects quickly, or if the objects have become so wet and dirty they won't like to take them into their mouths. In due course, we should be able to train out these small hang-ups, but only through motivation and fun, and above all in separate training sessions.

And another thing: in some areas, you may not be welcome when you lay out your search objects and have your dog dash about the open countryside searching for them. You should ask for the land-owner's or gamekeeper's permission (if there is one), especially when working with substitute game. Please also bear in mind there may be particular seasons when or places where you should not train, or in fact are not allowed to do so. There are

Pick an area for your search which has varied terrain features that are appropriate for your dog's training status.

many areas where you're legally obliged to keep your dog on a lead during the breeding or nesting season, and you should respect these restrictions. There are enough other areas and possibilities where you and your dog can have fun snooping all year round, so why annoy people and other animals if you don't have to?

This is important to know:

- If you're using several search objects at the same time, these should be similar and of equal value.
- Choose a terrain that suits your dog's training level.
- Never allow your dog to work with a lead and collar in broken or difficult terrain.
- Pay attention to the wind direction.
- Take into account the weather conditions.

From search apprentice to journeyman

We begin with a very easy exercise. First off, this is about learning the vocabulary. Our dog should get to know the audio and visual signs for the blind retrieve. The word 'search' and a wide sweeping arm gesture are the usual starting aids for this search work in particular. Let's use them as an example. We opt for dummies as search objects.

Always acquaint your dog with the search object right at the beginning. He is supposed to enjoy carrying it around. If this is not the case, you can train retrieving with your dog before embarking on this search task. Should you need to, you can read up on how this can be done through a fun but systematic approach, near the beginning of the book.

For the first blind retrieve, have your dog sit at the margins of a small, but not too overgrown search area. This could be your garden, or a lawn in a park. Take a single dummy and lay it out carefully. If he can see it lying in the grass, this is not a problem, but it's not necessary either. Stand next to your dog, wait a brief moment, and then send him on the search with an encouraging 'search' and the wide sweeping arm gesture. You must wait three to four seconds, before sending him off – this builds up the tension while at the same time serving as impulse control training. As always, what's expected in this situation is for your dog to learn to wait until you give him the signal for action.

Repeat this exercise several times in various different types of terrain. After a few repetitions, you should no longer lay out the dummies in such a way that your dog can see them lying there, as otherwise he will get used to just searching with his eyes and this is exactly what we're trying to avoid. If your dog tends to primarily use his eyes anyway, you should avoid areas with very short vegetation right from the start. Dogs who primarily rely on their vision have to realise as

Lucy heads off after the word 'search' and the relevant arm gesture.

Two decoy pigeons have been installed to distract and mislead, but Lucy ignores them.

She searches and finds the dummy without hesitation ...

... and immediately takes it to her owner.

Always conclude a training unit by letting the dog fetch for fun and with a joint playing session.

quickly as possible that they will only reach their goal if they use their sense of smell.

As soon as you're aware that your dog has understood what the blind retrieve is all about, you can use several dummies. At this point, it may be important to decide what colour the dummies should be, depending on the training requirement or the type of dog. Let us recall: blue-green and white dummies are visible to the dog, orange ones are almost invisible.

After repeating this first step several times, lay out the dummies without the dog being able to see you do it. Once again, let's begin with just one dummy and in a simple kind of terrain, but even at this early stage you should also work towards your dog using his nose in order to find the dummy.

You should pay attention to the wind conditions as well. At the beginning, you should make use of a headwind. By doing this you're making your dog's task a lot easier. Later you should also train with a sidewind. A tailwind turns every search task into a challenge, but it also teaches him a good search style, and helps prevent one frequently made mistake: The dog is not supposed to take any clues from the tracks we've left behind when we were laying out the search objects, because he is supposed to search only for the dummies. In order to achieve this, throw the dummies into the search area in a semi-circle, throwing them in the direction of the wind. This way he won't find any dummies, if all he does is follow your tracks.

It is important for every dog to learn how to work with the wind. This means that he should always work against the wind, which means having to search the terrain in large loops. If the wind blows from the left, we should send the dog to the right with a slight turn of our body and a sweeping gesture.

On a large scale search, a dog with a good search style works with his nose in the air, and in wide arches. He will cover the search area as thoroughly as possible.

If you have laid out several dummies, it is important that the dog is greatly motivated to carry out the search until the last dummy has been found. Here are a few tricks that will help you achieve this. As soon as he has brought one dummy, you should send him off again straight after he has handed it over, without having him sit beforehand. Make a point of remembering which dummies he has retrieved, so you know where the last dummy is located. For the last one you should always go on the 'search' together with him. This way he quickly learns: as long as my human does not enter the search area with me, there are enough dummies out there for me to find. Make sure you let him pick up the last dummy himself and carry it back to the start line.

Every object the dog brings to you should immediately be put away in a bag, so it doesn't distract the dog from his next search. Never leave the found objects on the ground behind, or next to you.

Increase the number of search objects only gradually, and stop before your dog loses interest. Should this ever happen, it's best to conclude the training unit by letting him fetch something just for fun, or use the search object to play with him. This will build up your dog's motivation for the next training unit.

Incidentally, it is entirely possible that the dummies or other objects that your dog may bring to you will be wet, filthy or covered in mud. You should nevertheless accept them with good grace, as if they had just emerged fresh from the washing machine. Otherwise your dog may end up treating this piece with disgust as well, or develop similar sensitivities regarding dirt, and as a result may decide not to bring you such filthy objects.

If your dog does not possess the best of noses, something which is fairly common in short-nosed dogs, you can still work with scents, especially out in the open. This makes it easier to find a search object in amongst all the lovely smells in the countryside. Popular scents include aniseed oil or camomile.

From journeyman to master snooper

The only way your dog will become a master snooper is through training with you. Almost every dog has a huge potential regarding the ability to find things with his nose. The blind retrieve offers countless opportunities. If your dog is an ad-

Jasper has to stick his nose deep into the tall grass and concentrate hard in order to find the little ball.

vanced snooper, you can structure the most interesting searches in almost any type of terrain.

From now on, on no account should you assist your dog if he doesn't find the search object straight away and is asking you for help. Turn away from him, thus signalling he should trust his nose instead of relying on your assistance.

In future, you should also work with a tailwind more often. Your dog is supposed to run deep into the search area in order to 'catch the wind'. Allow him to find his own search style by trial and error. You should increasingly send him into difficult terrain with higher or unattractive vegetation. Include meadows as well as thick covers or ditches, and keep changing between different types of terrain.

To make things more difficult for your dog, you could also start using different objects, such as smaller ones, instead of the usual search objects. Tennis balls, for example, are difficult to find, being smaller than standard dummies. To make things more exciting, you can pick colours that your dog cannot see very well such as orange. A small 100 g orange dummy that has been put in a ditch – you will need a fully-fledged snooping expert to find that! And when he has to search for more than one of these dummies, one after the other – and finds them – both team partners can be pleased with themselves. Good work!

Night shift for bright things

You can get a real kick out of a blind retrieve, if you structure the search in the dark. In winter especially, we have little choice other than to carry out our evening walks by torchlight. If your dog is working and obeying reliably, why not have him conduct a search in the dark?

Have the dog sit, and disappear into the darkness. Throw the dummies or other search objects away from you so your dog can't just follow your tracks in order to get to them. Then return to him, and send him on the search. If your dog has a luminous collar, you'll be able to see him busily rushing through the night, while listening out for his breathing and his footfalls. This is really exciting for both of you. At the beginning, most dogs will occasionally stop in their tracks during a search in order to ascertain whether you're still there or where exactly you are. They will listen out and try to catch sight of you.

Initially your dog may experience problems finding his way back to you, because he is not yet able to find his bearings very well. You have to observe him closely and listen carefully in order to keep track of his movements. Help him find his way back to you by clearing your throat or calling him. You will see that after repeating this a few times, you won't need to do it anymore. Our dogs don't take long to get used to working in the dark.

Apart from the fun, this experience provides you with an important additional bonus: you both learn to rely on each other. Blind. Without any light.

Dragging and tracking

There is one piece of nose work in the context of dragging and tracking that requires our dogs to use a totally different approach than the previous snooping tasks.

Up to now, the search objective was to cover large areas; but now the dog is supposed to learn to systematically follow a long trail with his nose. In nature, we usually come across game tracks or the tracks of other dogs. Anyone who is used to closely observing their dog during walks will be aware that he often randomly picks up and follows some tracks. We have no way of knowing where they begin and where they might end. It is exactly this that creates problems for so many owners, because once the dog has got into snooping mode, he doesn't see or hear anything else – he's off.

With the help of the tasks presented here, we'll set up a controlled situation, and train the systematic working of an interesting trail. This will happen on command, however, which puts the work that our dog loves under signal control. This way you are able to experience one of your dog's favourite leisure pursuits together with him, instead of your dog having all the fun.

For the dragging work you'll need:

- A drag line and harness
- Some hot dog pieces and thinned-down brine
- A bottle or freezer bags for drizzling
- A dummy, toy, scented tube or a dragging object of your choice
- Marking aids: marking tape (available from fieldsport/pet supplies retailers), laundry pegs and paper tissues, or a notepad and pen to make notes.

The hot dog drag

A hot dog drag is the perfect start for drag training. You need some small (but not too small) hot dog pieces, some brine, a drag line, about five- to ten-metres long, and a harness. Dilute the brine by adding some tap water. For drizzling water, you can

A good recipe for the first steps of the drag training; hot dogs and hot dog brine.

use a freezer bag with a tiny hole pierced in the bottom, or a plastic bottle with a pull-out drinking nozzle.

As an alternative to hot dogs and brine, you can also use boiled chicken, cut up into small pieces, and chicken broth.

Have your dog wear a harness while dragging, in order to protect his neck – because for a change he is allowed, and even supposed to pull lightly on the line.

The first steps

Choose a simple terrain – short grass or tarmac is a good surface for the first drag. It is best to work against the wind, in order to enable the dog to achieve a quick success.

Put two pieces of hot dog on the start line of the drag. This is where the hot dog drag or scent trail begins, and you continue to lay in a straight line. Put small pieces of hot dog on the drag in short regular intervals. You should conclude the first few drags with a little jackpot after about 20 metres: lay out several small hot dog pieces there. Your dog should not see this jackpot too soon, because otherwise he will learn to use his eyes rather than his nose. This is something we want to avoid.

There is one important principle regarding the end of a drag; here the dog ought to find the very object whose scent he has been following with his nose. So don't lay out a toy or chicken pieces at

Put some pieces of hot dog and a splash of hot dog brine on the start line of the drag.

Show the start line to the dog. Balou finds this spot very interesting.

the end of a drag, when it is a trail of hot dog brine that has got him there. This would give him a mixed message: you don't always find what you're looking for. This kind of thing would confuse a dog as much as it would confuse us, and he might draw the wrong conclusions from what he has just learned.

To begin with, let the dog watch you once or twice while you structure the task. Have

him sit down a short distance away, then lay the drag as described above. Wait a few minutes to give the scent a chance to develop.

Then begin with a ritual which from now on you will use at the start of every drag: Lead the dog close to the start line and have him sit down a few metres away from it. Examine the ground and show an interest in that particular spot.

With his nose on the ground he is sniffing his way from hot dog to hot dog all the way to the jackpot.

Next, get your dog and show him the start line. Say 'drag' in a quiet, but encouraging voice, or a different command. Make sure that there is a clear distinction between this and the search command for the blind retrieve, because this type of work is fundamentally different. Your gestures should not be the same either.

Let him eat the first hot dog pieces and follow the hot dog brine drag. Always keep the line slightly tightened, but don't pull on it.

If your dog loses the drag, coax him back a small distance and get him to start afresh at the point where he left the trail, then let him get back into snooping mode once more. Don't say no, and don't withdraw either. At the beginning, if nothing else will work, you can help him by pointing to the drag with your hand, or by making rustling noises in the grass where it is. Eventually he will find the jackpot, thus motivating him to repeat the exciting exercise. At the beginning, you shouldn't let him run more than two or three short drags in a row.

Hold the drag line firmly, but not too firmly with both hands. It should always be slightly tight, but only when the dog is moving forward. Never pull or jerk on the line.

With each repetition, the hot dog trail we lay out gets longer. Increase the distance between the hot dog pieces steadily, until eventually you don't put any pieces on the start line and on the drag any more, but only at the finish. Don't keep doing short and easy drags for too long, because dogs can get bored easily. Begin training with a sidewind as well. A headwind might tempt a dog into 'swinging', where he moves forward with swerving movements, sometimes to the right and sometimes to the left of the drag. This could easily turn into a blind retrieve. And of course this is not what we want. That's why you should take advantage of a sidewind as soon as possible. The dog will throw himself into the wind a little, and as a result no longer walk precisely on the drag. The stronger the wind, the further the dog will work parallel to the drag. This can easily be as much as one or two metres.

At this point the time is right for including some slight angles. Initially you should use angles that are larger than 90 degrees. Only advanced dogs should work with angles smaller than 90 degrees. In order to help your dog during the first training units lay out a hot dog piece directly before and after the angle respectively.

Now observe your dog. He will overshoot the angle more than once, then stop in his tracks, go back, make sure he has sniffed correctly, and then get back on the drag. You can see him think: 'that's very exciting'.

If he doesn't know what to do next, help him. Walk a few metres back along the drag and show him where he can pick it up again, just in case he can't find it by himself. As you can see, your senses and powers of concentration are also much in demand.

This type of nose work requires a lot of effort on the part of the dog. However, it suits his talents and that's why he will quickly pick it up. After only a few repetitions, he knows what to do. Always bear in mind that this is exactly what your dog is best at – following trails.

Dragging for expert sniffers

It won't take long before you can call your dog a dragging expert. Now you can start his advanced training.

Lay out the drag across various different terrain surfaces – for example, from a short-cut lawn across a path, and then onto a meadow with higher grass. Deliberately mislead your dog by adding decoys in the shape of other drags (for example toy drags, made by pulling a toy on a string across the ground), that go across the hot dog drag, or put objects next to the drag which your dog is supposed to ignore.

At this point you should also start working with a tailwind. This is very difficult for the dog, and requires the highest degree of concentration. Make sure that to begin with the wind is not too strong. With a tailwind the dog will quickly get used to working with his nose on the ground. This is important because it enables him to pick up the scent of the drag and avoid being distracted by other scents.

For a change, you could also put the search object on a tree stump or a wall. Observe your dog's baffled expression when the drag suddenly stops, but somehow the scent is still in the air! This kind of surprise keeps the training fresh and interesting.

Gradually extend the time that the drag stands idle – this is the period between the drag being laid and the dog working on it – up to several hours. Once more, take into account the weather conditions as well. At an advanced training stage, if there are normal temperatures with a light wind, you can leave a drag to stand idle for up to two hours without any problem. Scorching sunshine and dry conditions, on the other hand, would make the scent evaporate too

What a surprise! The drag ends, but the scent is in the air. Goya finds the dummy on the hedge.

quickly, so that the dog may not be able to perform the task any more after the same amount of time has passed.

You can gradually extend the drags to several hundred metres. There are exams where dogs work drags of more than one kilometre. After regular training, our dogs will be able to do this too.

When working with longer and more complicated routes, it may be a good idea to draw a map of the drag route or to mark it while laying it. To mark the route you can attach strips of paper tissues, clothes pegs or paper-marking tape (available for this purpose from dog sports retailers) to tree branches. Particularly where a change of direction is involved, you should mark this in such a way that you can easily spot whether your dog is still on the drag, and you can help him if necessary.

Only ever increase the level of difficulty regarding one individual factor. If you opt for a terrain that is more difficult than the one you had used previously, don't simultaneously extend the route, or the time span during which the drag is left to stand idle.

And don't forget to offer your dog some water, especially after a long marathon drag.

The weather has a strong influence on the drag:

- High temperatures and very low temperatures make the nose work much harder.
- If there is no wind at all the scent almost settles on the drag.
- Strong winds blow the scent away, usually only in one direction.
- Frost limits the development of the scent.

Goya is allowed to watch for a moment as his owner drags the dummy along. She (and the dummy) will turn off at the bush. Goya will have to use his nose from there.

Dummy, scent tubes, food dummy and toy drags

If your dog has understood the principles of dragging, there are many future opportunities for interesting search tasks for him. You can lay dummy, toy, food dummy or scent-tube drags. It is certainly amazing how confidently our dogs will find all these objects by working the drag.

The objects should not be too light so they have sufficient impact on the terrain when you drag them across the ground on a rope. Always walk on the lee side, away from the wind, to avoid your tracks being blown across the drag. Otherwise your dog will quickly learn to follow your tracks rather than the scent of the drag object. If you want to avoid this completely, you should lay out the drag with a dog sport fishing rod. Tie the drag object to the fishing rod.

If the wind comes from the left side, walk as far to the right of the drag as possible, and drag the object along.

With his nose on the ground he follows the drag all the way to the dummy ...

... and returns it to his owner.

If you have a dog who you're certain will come back to you, there is no reason why he shouldn't work long drags without a line. In a hunting context, it would not be unusual to expect this from a well-trained hunting dog. At the end there should always be an object that your dog can retrieve and bring back to you. Marking would only be possible by barking or, for expert snoopers, through the Bringsel indication, because the dog will disappear from view. For safety reasons, the dog should work without a collar wherever there is a risk that he might get entangled.

Should this be necessary, you can also train drags with game substitutes, in case your dog is only interested in game scents rather than in standard dummies or toys. A dragged hare fur dummy that has also been imbued with artificial hare smell will make any dog with a strong hunting instinct very keen. Nevertheless, I would like to emphasise once again that it is important to divert the dog's interests onto

This drag is laid with a dog sport fishing rod in order to ensure that the dog follows the dummy drag and not our tracks. (Photo: M. Nau)

more 'harmless' drags as soon as possible. If your dog is galloping across a meadow or emerging from a wood with a rabbit fur dummy in his teeth, this might easily lead to misunderstandings. In addition, we want to divert his interest away from pursuing game altogether.

We combine:
Exciting snooping tasks

And what are we going to do after our dog is able to do all those things we've been discussing so far? We can create exciting combinations of various different tasks – our imagination has no bounds. We will stick with dummies because dogs love to carry and search for them, they have a sufficient scent of their own, they are available in many different sizes, and also because when training with several objects simultaneously it's better for all the objects to look the same. Of course, you can go for other search objects as well; however do make sure your dog is completely clued up about what he is supposed to look for.

For example, an assistant could throw a dummy on a string in full view. We call this tagging. At the beginning you should opt for a terrain which is not too difficult. The assistant drags the dummy on the string away across the ground. Have your dog watch this for a short while. While the dummy is finally disappearing behind a high bush or into tall grass, briefly distract him. How far the assistant should drag the dummy depends on the training status of the dog.

Now you send the dog to retrieve the dummy. When he arrives at the spot where the dummy touched down, he will stop short, because the dummy has gone! You can help him by calling the command for the drag, or you can leave it up to him, how he will find the dummy. Depending on the type of dog and his training status, you have to decide how to carry on from here. If your dog has found the dummy, both of you have done something really momentous.

In the course of the training the drags will have to cover a longer distance. You should lay the drag first, without the dog watching you. It could well be several hundred metres long. At the end you leave the dragged dummy (not a different one!) on the ground. Now get the dog, let him watch while the assistant throws the tag, turn the dog the other way, and have him fetch a dummy that has been laid out or thrown earlier. This is how you distract him. Meanwhile, the assistant takes away the thrown dummy. Now you turn the dog around again, and send him to find the dummy that has escaped from the dog's field of vision and whose drag he is now supposed to work on. To manage tasks like these together does not just require a lot of knowledge and skill, but also trust and teamwork.

The next task also becomes more interesting if you have the help of an assistant. Lay out a blind retrieve with one or several dummies, without your dog watching you. Then take up your position with your dog, and have him sit next to your feet. You (or an assistant) lays out or throws a dummy at an angle of 180 degrees, with your back to the search terrain. However, the dog is not allowed to fetch this immediately. Instead you turn around and send him on the search that has been laid out beforehand. Once he has brought you the dummy he is allowed to fetch the visibly laid or thrown out dummy. This exercise includes stationary calm, obedience and lots of anticipation.

These are only three examples of how we can combine different tasks with each other. Of course the easiest way to do these tasks would be without a drag line; therefore the dog should be generally

You and your dog will have a lot of fun, even when managing some more difficult tasks.

obedient and not embark on private excursions while you're waiting for him.

As a result, you should be able to structure some interesting training sessions. You will find you will be able to think of ever new variations, perhaps with different objects or in combination with working in water – at a lake, for instance. You and your dog will have a lot of fun carrying out these tasks together, including difficult ones as well.

'Find the human!'– tracking training

If our dog enjoys working on drags, he will also be sure to like sniffing out tracks. A track is – or is usually described as – a succession of imprints on the ground, made by vehicles, animals or human beings. In other words, it's something that has made an impact on the ground. If somebody or something impacts on the ground, plants and tiny life forms are squashed. These dissolve into their components, gas is emitted, and this is what our dogs can smell. In addition, tiny particles fall off our shoes, or dead skin cells are shed from our bodies every second of our lives – humans in particular keep flaking all the time. An experienced dog will be able to find us without any problem, wherever we are. Let's have a look how we can teach this to our dog.

For the tracking training you need:

- A drag line
- A harness
- Treats or toys
- Marking aids or a notepaper and pen.

We are tracking

We'll start with our own tracks. In the first instance, your dog is supposed to learn to search for you.

While we make the following preparations, have the dog lie down some distance away, and let him observe you. This will arouse his curiosity and increase his motivation.

Once again, begin with a headwind. Just as regarding drags, this only applies to the first tracking exercises – after that you should opt for a sidewind and then quickly go for a tailwind. First off, begin with a light breeze. Otherwise the same weather rules for dragging apply to tracking as well.

Before laying the trail, plan the route the track should follow. At the beginning, the terrain should not be too difficult.

Mark the start line for yourself. Firmly stamp on it several times with your shoe. Lay two or three treats into these shoe prints, so your dog will find this spot particularly exciting. Next, walk along leaving your tracks behind. For the first few tracks put a treat into the first few of your footprints. Walk in a straight line and not too far away. At the end, a jackpot awaits the dog – put several treats into the last footprint that you want your dog to reach. Afterwards, carry on walking for a few paces before returning to the dog in the direction of the wind (not against it).

Wait a few minutes before having your dog start from the start line. In the mean-time, do something else with him. Most dogs will remember what they had observed a few minutes ago, and will be pleased to see what you've been up to.

Now you perform the same rituals as you did at the beginning of the drag. Put the dog on a drag line and have him sit down a few metres away. Then examine the start line, afterwards take your expert snooper there, show him the spot, let him have a treat, and encourage him to follow your tracks. While he is getting on his way, you can introduce a new command right at the beginning. This could be 'track', for example.

Have the dog work the track on a slightly tightened lead. If he loses it, you can help him by stopping, and going back a few metres, or at the beginning also by pointing to the track once more. Do show him with your hands where he is supposed to start sniffing. At the end of the track a jackpot awaits him.

Tracks for expert sniffers

You will find that after just a few tracks you can increase the level of difficulty. Work in more difficult wind conditions, across various types of terrain, longer dis-

tances, obtuse angles above 90 degrees, and with longer stand and wait times.

In order to always know a bit more than your dog, mark the route or make some notes on a piece of paper while walking. Before heading off, you should identify some landmarks in the terrain as targets, otherwise you can easily get lost whilst laying the track. For example, walk from a large tree in a straight line to a large rock, then turn right and walk towards a cut-down tree trunk, where you carry on straight ahead to the first bush.

Armed with these notes you can have your dog climb over obstacles such as felled trees, you can lay false trails with artificial scents, or another person lays a false track that crosses your track either beforehand or afterwards.

But what do we do if the dog leaves the correct track, and follows one of the false trails instead? Stop and don't say anything at first. Then go back until your dog can sniff out the point where the two tracks cross. Only help him if he is completely at a loss. It would be better if he were to find out by himself what went wrong. You should follow him only once he has picked up the right track again. As long as this is not the case, stay where you are, or – if there is no other way – show him where the correct track is running.

However, in the long term it will become boring for our dog to sniff out our own tracks, no matter how interesting we try to make it. Because of that, and since we want him to become smarter all the time, at some point we should start to have him search for other people as well. If we want to make this new task easier for him, we can let him sniff scent samples from that person's items of (worn) clothing. This will give him that person's idiosyncratic scent in addition to their tracks. This person would have spread millions of dead skin cells around their tracks while he laid the track, which will be of additional help to your dog in order to reach his goal with confidence.

And you thought that one couldn't possibly take this any further? But yes! You can lay tracks in an urban environment too. After all, it doesn't have to be the central shopping area on a Saturday afternoon. Slightly calmer side streets would do the job also, and there would certainly be enough distractions. You shouldn't just walk along the pavement, but instead cross from one side of the road to the other in order to avoid a fenced-off area, or go into a shop and out again. Once again don't let the track stand idle for too long. Five minutes should be enough, bearing in mind the level of distraction present in this setting.

A brief exchange of eye contact before the start, and the search is on.

To conclude

In the course of this book we have covered a wide range of activities, from small 60-second snooping games to structured and demanding nose work. Discover the excitement you might have with developing and modifying these exercises in the future.

Nose work is a pursuit your dog will always be interested in, as long as there are new things to be discovered.

I wish you and your canine partner a lot of fun with this – and good luck in your search!

Further reading

You will probably want to read more about some of the subjects touched upon. Here you will find a great deal of interesting information:

Albrecht, Kat
Dog Detectives:
How to Train Your Dog to
Find Lost Pets
Dogwise, 2010

Charleson, Susannah
Scent of Missing: Love and Partnership
with a Search-And-Rescue Dog
Houghton Mifflin Harcourt, 2010

Hallgren, Anders
Mental Activation: Ways to Stimulate
Your Dog's Brain and Avoid Boredom
Cadmos, 2007

Liebeck, Christiane
Main-trailing:
How to Train Your Bloodhound
Cadmos, 2008

Mienk, Angie
The Invisible Link to Your Dog:
A New Way of Achieving Harmony
Between Dogs and Humans
Cadmos, 2011

Gutmann, Monika
Line Training for Dogs:
How it's done
Cadmos, 2009

Roder, Nicole
Whose Sofa is it Anyway?
A light-hearted look at training pitfalls
and how to avoid them
Cadmos, 2009

Supplier of scent tubes:

Hund und Freizeit e.K.
Uhlenbrock 10
49586 Neuenkirchen
Germany
www.hund-und-freizeit.com

Andreas Nau
Hundetrainingsartikel
Im Huck 10
47533 Kleve
Germany

Thanks ...

... to everybody who was involved in helping us create this great book about fun activities we can do together with our dogs. In particular, I would like to thank all the two-legged and four-legged photo models. You participated joyfully and with a lot of patience! I think it shows too.

The author

Martina Nau lives with her three dogs in the Lower Rhine region. For many years, she has been running her own dog school, where she offers courses in upbringing and activity, one-to-one training and anti-hunting training for family and hunting dogs. Her books and articles in professional publications are based on linking theory with practical experience.

(Photo: JBTierfoto)

Index

CADMOS
DOG GUIDES

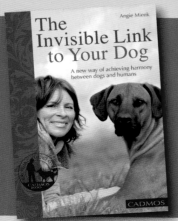

Angie Mienk

THE INVISIBLE LINK TO YOUR DOG

Times when dogs were trained to be only obedient or to carry out cer tasks are long gone. Many dog owners today wish to have a relation based on mutual understanding and a much closer bond to their four friend. This book presents a unique method that will help readers dev non-verbal, almost intuitive communication with their dogs.

80 pages, full colour, Softcover
ISBN 978-0-85788-201-1

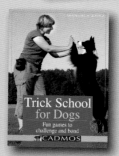

Manuela Zaitz

TRICK SCHOOL FOR DOGS

Everybody can give a dog a good mental or physical work-out at home or during a daily walk with the use of dog tricks. This book presents fun and challenging tricks to keep a dog eager and interested. Numerous photos make the practical application of tasks and exercises simple and en-courage readers to 'try this at home'.

128 pages, full colour, Softcover
ISBN 978-3-86127-960-0

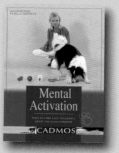

Anders Hallgren

MENTAL ACTIVATION

Dogs need to encounter and overcome physical and mental challenges to remain stimulated, happy and well. Anders Hallgren describes many simple ex-ercises designed to engage and improve a dog's senses. 'A wealth of fun ideas for increasing the interaction between you and your dog.' – Your Dog.

96 pages, full colour, Softcover
ISBN 978-3-86127-927-3

Monika Gutmann

MORE FUN WITH CLICKER TRAINING

Clicker training is the modern way of dog training and up-bringing. Anyone can learn this popular and animal-friend-ly training method, which is particularly good for develop-ing your dog's initiative. In addition to basic knowledge regarding clicker training, this book puts great emphasis on how to communicate clearly with dogs. Easy-to-follow exer-cises and practical tips for correcting undesired behav-iour enable the reader to make best use of the clicker marker signal.

96 pages, full colour, Softcover
ISBN 978-3-86127-983-9

Christina Sondermann

PLAYTIME FOR YO DOG

This book will help you dis and employ games and ac on an everyday basis that you and your dog will enjo that will contribute toward fitness and training: Marve the super-abilities of your sense of smell. Make his d walks an exciting adventur Find enough inspiration in living room to exercise his play instincts. With step-by illustrations.

128 pages, full colour, Hardc
ISBN 978-3-86127-922-8

For more information, please visit:
www.cadmos.co.uk

CADMOS